2107

D0754753

Map It!™

# PHYSICAL MAPS

Ian F. Mahaney

The Rosen Publishing Group's

PowerKids Press™

New York

*To my parents, who still deal with me daily*

Published in 2007 by The Rosen Publishing Group, Inc.
29 East 21st Street, New York, NY 10010

First Edition

Editor: Jennifer Way
Book Design: Greg Tucker
Photo Researcher: Jeffrey Wendt

Photo Credits: Cover, pp. 6, 10, 13, 14, 17, 18, 21 Library of Congress Geography and Map Division; pp. 5, 9 National Atlas of the United States, http://nationalatlas.gov.

Library of Congress Cataloging-in-Publication Data

Mahaney, Ian F.
  Physical maps / Ian F. Mahaney.— 1st ed.
      p. cm. — (Map it!)
  Includes index.
  ISBN 1-4042-3054-8 (library binding) — ISBN 1-4042-2210-3 (paperback)
  1. Maps—Juvenile literature. I. Title. II. Series.

  GA151.M267 2006
  912'.01'4—dc22

                                     2004025430

Manufactured in the United States of America

# Contents

# What Is a Map?

Do you know how to read a map? A map **represents** an area. The area a map shows can be large, like the world, or small, like a town. Maps use **symbols**, colors, and lines to give facts about the area they represent.

Though they show different things, all maps have a few things in common. All maps have a **compass rose**, which shows the four main directions. These directions are north, south, east, and west. Every map has a **legend**, which explains the symbols on the map. All maps also have a **scale**, which explains the difference between distances on the map and distances in the real world. In this book you will learn all that you need to know about reading and understanding a physical map.

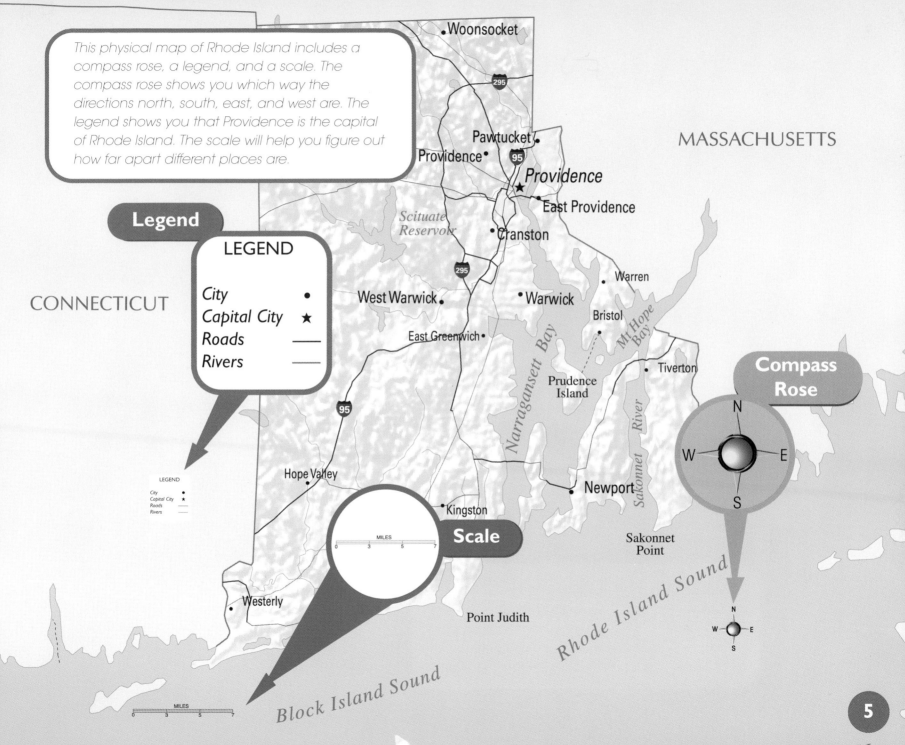

This physical map of Rhode Island includes a compass rose, a legend, and a scale. The compass rose shows you which way the directions north, south, east, and west are. The legend shows you that Providence is the capital of Rhode Island. The scale will help you figure out how far apart different places are.

**Legend**

LEGEND

City     •
Capital City     ★
Roads     ——
Rivers     ——

**Compass Rose**

**Scale**

MILES
0   3   5   7

MASSACHUSETTS

CONNECTICUT

Woonsocket

Pawtucket
Providence
Providence
East Providence
Cranston

Scituate Reservoir

West Warwick
Warwick
Warren
Bristol
East Greenwich
Mt Hope Bay
Tiverton
Prudence Island
Narragansett Bay
Sakonnet River

Hope Valley

Newport
Kingston
Sakonnet Point

Westerly
Point Judith

Block Island Sound

Rhode Island Sound

OCEAN

On this physical map of the continental United States, you can see natural features. The different colors used on the map show the features. For example, bodies of water are shades of blue and different types of forests are shades of green.

# What Is a Physical Map?

A physical map shows an area's natural features. Oceans, rivers, and mountains are examples of natural features. If the area where you live is near mountains, you can use a physical map to find the names and locations of those mountains. Physical maps may also include major humanmade features, such as the capital cities of states and countries and the **political borders** between states and countries.

Physical maps show natural and humanmade features by using different symbols and colors. They also show the **relief** of certain **landforms**, such as mountains, deserts, and forests. Different colors on a physical map may point out features such as forests or deserts. The map's legend will help you figure out what the symbols and colors on a physical map mean.

# Basic Map Symbols and Colors

The legend is one of the most important things for you to understand when reading a physical map. The legend shows the different symbols, colors, and shapes that are used on the map. Three different kinds of symbols are used on physical maps. Point symbols show certain points, such as cities. Cities are marked with a black dot. Area symbols represent larger areas, such as lakes, deserts, and forests. Line symbols show things such as rivers and political borders.

Physical maps also use colors to help point out features. For example, forest and wetland areas might appear in shades of green. Water is always colored blue. The legend on each map that you read will tell you what colors, shapes, and symbols are used on the map.

Look at the legend on this physical map of the United States. It shows that lakes are blue on the map. Can you find Lake Michigan? The legend also shows that capital cities are stars, but that other cities are dots. Look at the state of North Dakota. Which city is the capital, Bismarck or Fargo?

**LEGEND**

| | |
|---|---|
| City | ● |
| Capital City | ★ |
| Road | — |
| Freeway | 〔95〕 |
| River | — |
| Lake | ▬ |

Albers equal area projection

0    100    200    300 mi
0  100  200  300 km

Chicago

New York

W   N   E

S

The compass rose on this physical map shows the four basic directions, which are north, south, east, and west. Find the cities of New York and Chicago. Trace your finger from New York City to Chicago. By looking at the compass rose, you can see that Chicago is west in relation to New York City.

# Which Way Is Which?

If you look at the map of the United States on the opposite page, you will see that the compass rose is marked with an N on the top, an S on the bottom, an E on the right, and a W on the left. These are the four main directions, north, south, east, and west. These directions allow us to **describe** the locations of two places in **relation** to each other.

If you look at the map, you can see that Chicago is to the left of New York City. If you place your finger on New York City and trace a line to Chicago, you will be moving left on the map. Moving left on the map means you would be moving west in the real world. Another way to say this is that Chicago is west of New York City. Likewise New York City is east of Chicago.

Maps are smaller than the area they show. To show how distances on a map relate to distances in the world, mapmakers use a scale. The scale shows you that a certain distance on the map is equal to a certain distance in the world. For example, the scale may be labeled 1 inch = 1 mile (2.5 cm = 1.6 km). This means that 1 inch (2.5 cm) on the map is equal to one mile (1.6 km) in the world.

On a physical map, the most common type of scale used is a bar scale. A bar scale has a line with a bar at either end of the line. For example, you may see bar scales with one bar labeled 0 miles (0 km), and the second bar labeled 1 mile (1.6 km). This means that the length of the line on the map is equal to 1 mile (1.6 km) in the world.

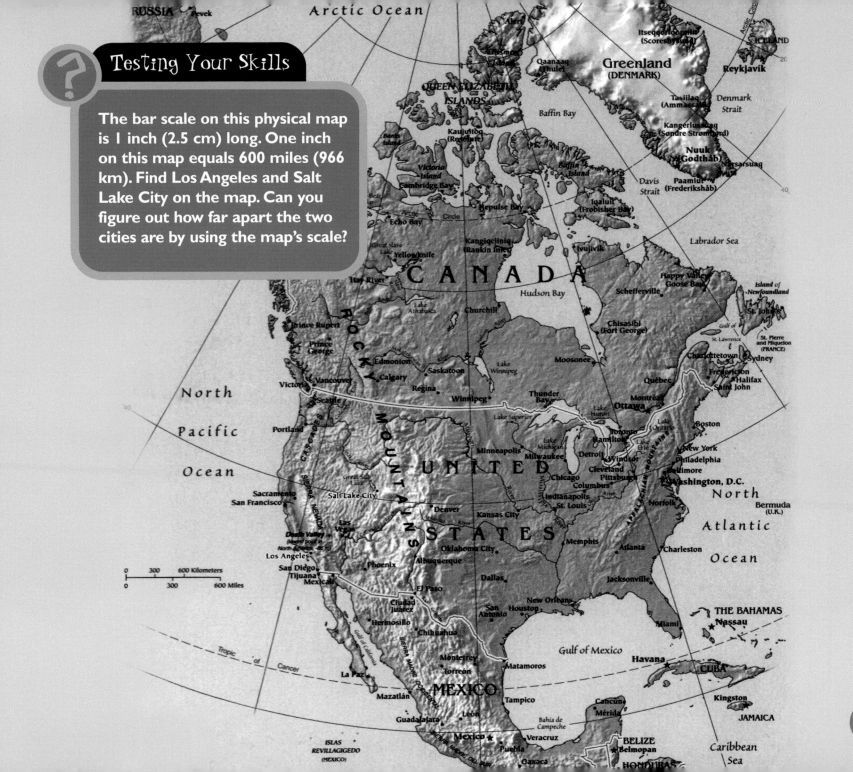

The bar scale on this physical map is 1 inch (2.5 cm) long. One inch on this map equals 600 miles (966 km). Find Los Angeles and Salt Lake City on the map. Can you figure out how far apart the two cities are by using the map's scale?

RUSSIA • Pevek

Arctic Ocean

Itseqqortoormiit
(Scoresbysund)

ICELAND

Greenland
(DENMARK)

Reykjavík

Qaanaaq
(Thule)

QUEEN ELIZABETH
ISLANDS

Baffin Bay

Tasiilaq
(Ammassalik)

Denmark
Strait

Kangerlussuaq
(Sondre Strømfjord)

Kaujuitoq
(Resolute)

Nuuk
(Godthåb)

Narsarsuaq

Banks
Island

Victoria
Island

Cambridge Bay

Baffin
Island

Davis
Strait

Paamiut
(Frederikshåb)

Iqaluit
(Frobisher Bay)

Repulse Bay

Labrador Sea

Echo Bay

Circle

Kangiqcliniq
(Rankin Inlet)

Ivujivik

Great Slave
Lake

Yellowknife

CANADA

Happy Valley
Goose Bay

Island of
Newfoundland

Scheffeville

Hay River

Churchill

Hudson Bay

Chisasibi
(Fort George)

St. John's

Lake
Athabasca

Gulf of
St. Lawrence

St. Pierre
and Miquelon
(FRANCE)

Prince Rupert

Prince
George

Edmonton

Saskatoon

Moosonee

Charlottetown

Sydney

Québec

Fredericton

Vancouver

Calgary

Lake
Winnipeg

Thunder
Bay

Montréal

Halifax
Saint John

Victoria

Regina

Winnipeg

Montréal

Ottawa

Boston

North

Seattle

Lake Superior

Lake
Huron

Toronto

Lake
Ontario

Portland

Minneapolis

Lake
Michigan

Milwaukee

Detroit

Windsor

Cleveland

Pittsburgh

New York

Philadelphia

Pacific

UNITED

Chicago

Columbus

Baltimore

Washington, D.C.

Sacramento

San Francisco

Great Salt
Lake

Salt Lake City

STATES

Indianapolis

St. Louis

Norfolk

North

Ocean

Denver

Kansas City

Bermuda
(U.K.)

Las
Vegas

Memphis

Atlantic

Death Valley
(lowest point in
North America, -86 m)

Los Angeles

Phoenix

Oklahoma City

Albuquerque

Atlanta

Charleston

Ocean

San Diego

Dallas

Jacksonville

0    300    600 Kilometers

Tijuana

Mexicali

El Paso

New Orleans

THE BAHAMAS

0    300    600 Miles

Ciudad
Juárez

San
Antonio

Houston

Miami

Nassau

Hermosillo

Chihuahua

Gulf of Mexico

Havana

CUBA

Tropic    of    Cancer

La Paz

Monterrey

Torreón

Matamoros

Kingston

Mazatlán

MEXICO

Tampico

Cancún

Mérida

JAMAICA

Guadalajara

León

Bahía de
Campeche

Veracruz

BELIZE

Belmopan

Caribbean

ISLAS
REVILLAGIGEDO
(MEXICO)

Mexico

Puebla

Oaxaca

HONDURAS

Sea

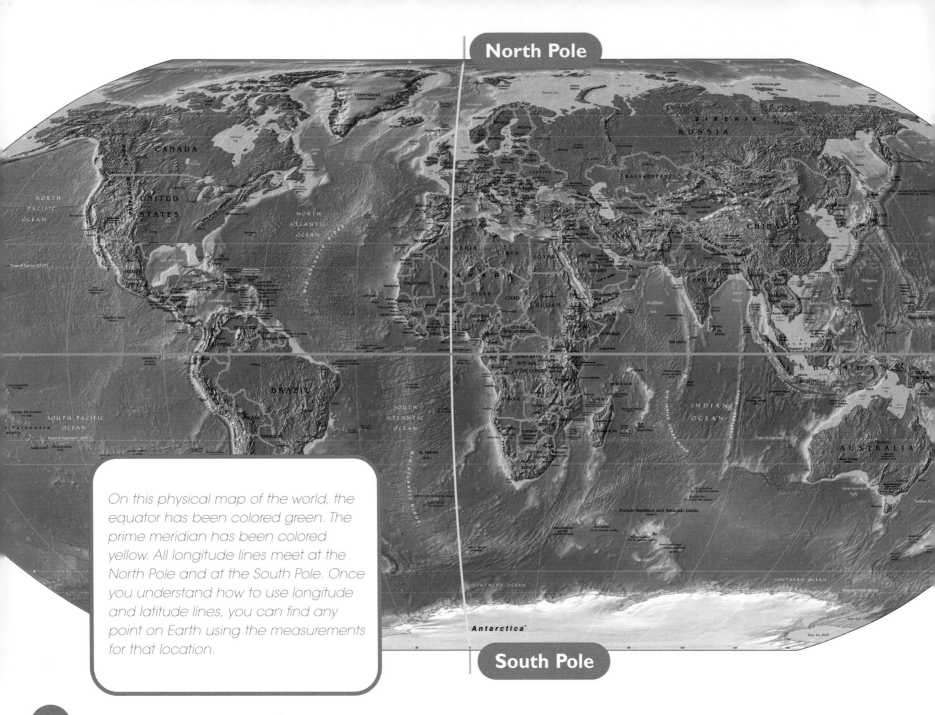

North Pole

South Pole

On this physical map of the world, the equator has been colored green. The prime meridian has been colored yellow. All longitude lines meet at the North Pole and at the South Pole. Once you understand how to use longitude and latitude lines, you can find any point on Earth using the measurements for that location.

# Measuring on Maps

Maps have special lines that help you locate places. **Longitude** lines run north and south, while **latitude** lines run east and west. The distances between longitude lines and latitude lines are measured in **degrees**. Every location on Earth can be described by a combination of a longitude and a latitude measurement.

There are also some special longitude and latitude lines on Earth. The **prime meridian** is 0° longitude. It separates the world's Eastern **Hemisphere** from the Western Hemisphere. The **equator** is 0° latitude. It separates the world into the Northern Hemisphere and the Southern Hemisphere. There are also two special points at the northernmost and the southernmost points in the world. All the longitude lines meet at these two points. The North Pole is the northernmost point. The South Pole is the southernmost point.

Water is shown in blue on physical maps. Using color makes it easy to figure out where bodies of water are on a map. Different bodies of water are represented in different ways on the map. On a physical map, rivers are blue, but they are also shown as a line symbol. Line symbols are included in the legend. Lakes are areas of blue surrounded on all sides by land. Bays and gulfs are bodies of water that are partly surrounded by land. The Gulf of Mexico and the Hudson Bay are examples of these bodies of water in North America. Seas are even larger. The Caribbean Sea is an example of a sea. The biggest bodies of water on Earth are called oceans.

Did you know that about three-quarters of the world is covered by water? When you look at a physical map of Earth, most of the map is blue.

This physical map of Central America and the Caribbean shows many different bodies of water. In the northwest corner of the map is the Gulf of Mexico. The Caribbean Sea is in the center of the map. There are two oceans on the map. The Pacific Ocean is in the southwest corner of the map, and the Atlantic Ocean is in the northeast corner of the map.

17

This physical map of the area around the Mediterranean Sea shows many different landforms. The continent of Europe is in the northern half of the map, and the continent of Africa is in the southern half of the map. Italy and Greece are countries that are peninsulas. Sicily is an island at the tip of the Italian peninsula.

# Looking at Landforms

Landforms are the natural features of Earth. Landforms are labeled on physical maps. If we look at a physical map of the world, the first landforms we see are **continents** and islands. Continents are the seven largest landmasses on Earth. A physical map of the world shows the seven continents. They are North America, South America, Europe, Asia, Africa, Australia, and Antarctica. Islands are smaller landmasses that are surrounded entirely by water. For example, the country of Cuba is an island, and the state of Hawaii is a chain of islands.

Continents can include landforms called **peninsulas**. A peninsula is land connected to the continent on one side and surrounded by water on the other three sides. The state of Florida is a peninsula. Entire countries can be peninsulas. Italy and Greece are examples of countries that are peninsulas.

# Mountains, Plains, Plateaus, and Valleys

When you look at a physical map, you can also see landforms, such as mountains, plains, **plateaus**, and valleys. Mountains are large landforms that are higher than the land surrounding them. Plains are very level, flat areas. The Great Plains in the United States is an example of a plain. Plateaus are raised plains, or very wide hills with large, flat tops. The Ozark Plateau is in Missouri, Arkansas, and Oklahoma.

Physical maps also show valleys. Valleys are low areas. Death Valley in California is an example of this type of low area. Often the height of the land is color coded in the legend. For example, high areas may be colored brown, and lower areas may be colored green.

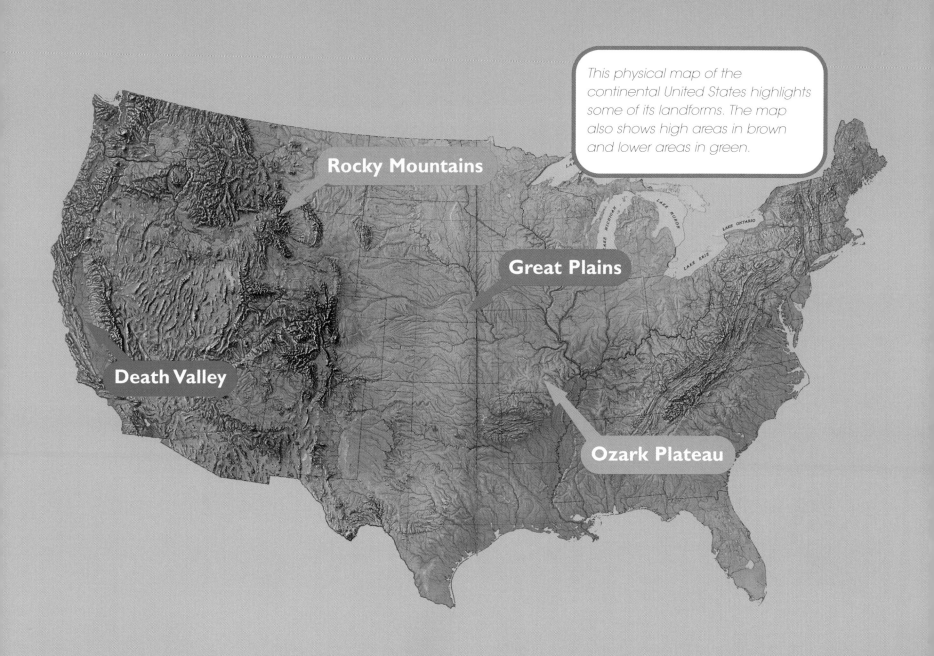

This physical map of the continental United States highlights some of its landforms. The map also shows high areas in brown and lower areas in green.

Rocky Mountains

Great Plains

Death Valley

Ozark Plateau

Physical maps provide us with an overview of the natural features and the major humanmade places in an area. Physical maps help us understand where different places are in relation to one another. You can use a physical map to figure out how far apart two cities are or to find out if the Rocky Mountains lie between those cities.

Physical maps do not give details such as how high mountains are or which roads you should take to travel between two cities. Physical maps are important because they give you a general idea about the land you are studying. Understanding the size, shape, and features of an area will help you understand more about that area and how it relates to the rest of the world.

# Glossary

**compass rose** (KUM-pus ROHZ)  A drawing on a map that shows directions.

**continents** (KON-teh-nents)  Earth's seven large landmasses.

**degrees** (dih-GREEZ)  Measurements of longitude and latitude.

**describe** (dih-SKRYB)  To explain.

**equator** (ih-KWAY-tur)  An imaginary line around Earth that separates it into two parts, northern and southern.

**hemisphere** (HEH-muh-sfeer)  One half of Earth or another sphere.

**landforms** (LAND-formz)  Features on Earth's surface, such as hills or valleys.

**latitude** (LA-tih-tood)  The distance north or south of the equator, measured by degrees.

**legend** (LEH-jend)  A box on a map that tells what the figures on the map mean.

**longitude** (LON-jih-tood)  The distance east or west of the prime meridian, measured by degrees.

**peninsulas** (peh-NIN-suh-luhz)  Areas of land surrounded by water on three sides.

**plateaus** (pla-TOHZ)  Broad, flat, high pieces of land.

**political borders** (puh-LIH-tih-kul BOR-durz)  The lines on a map between counties, states, or countries.

**prime meridian** (PRYM meh-RIH-dee-en)  The imaginary line that passes through Greenwich, England, and that is 0° longitude.

**relation** (rih-LAY-shun)  How something connects with something else.

**relief** (rih-LEEF)  The difference in height between two places.

**represents** (reh-prih-ZENTS)  Stands for.

**scale** (SKAYL)  The measurements on a map compared to actual measurements on Earth.

**symbols** (SIM-bulz)  Objects or pictures that stand for something else.

# Index

## C
compass rose, 4, 11
continent(s), 19

## D
Death Valley, 20

## E
Eastern Hemisphere, 15
equator, 15

## G
Great Plains, 20
Gulf of Mexico, 16

## H
Hudson Bay, 16

## L
landforms, 7, 19–20
latitude, 15
legend, 4, 7–8, 16, 20
longitude, 15

## N
Northern Hemisphere, 15

## O
Ozark Plateau, 20

## P
peninsula(s), 19
plateaus, 20
political borders, 7–8
prime meridian, 15

## R
relief, 7

## S
scale, 4, 12
Southern Hemisphere, 15

## W
Western Hemisphere, 15

# Web Sites

Due to the changing nature of Internet links, PowerKids Press has developed an online list of Web sites related to the subject of this book. This site is updated regularly. Please use this link to access the list:

www.powerkidslinks.com/mapit/physical/